THE MARRIAGE OF DAPHNIS AND CHLOE, 1959 wood engraving by Gwen Raverat. Closing scene showing the marriage of the noble shepherd and goatherdess on the island of Lesbos, from the pastoral love story Daphnis and Chloe, by the 2nd century Hellenistic romance writer Longus.

First published 2025
This edition © Amy Jones 2025

Published by Wooden Books Ltd.
Glastonbury, Somerset.
www.woodenbooks.com

British Library Cataloguing in Publication Data
Jones, A.
Genre & Trope

A CIP catalogue record for this book
may be obtained from the British Library.

ISBN-10: 1-907155-66-x
ISBN-13: 978-1-907155-66-6

All rights reserved.
For permission to reproduce any part of this
reassuring little book please contact the publishers.

Designed and typeset in Glastonbury, UK.
Printed in India on FSC® certified papers by
Quarterfold Printabilities Pvt. Ltd.

Genre & Trope

Amy Jones

Dedicated to writers everywhere.
With thanks to my editors Stephen Parsons & John Martineau.

Recommended further reading:
Genre, John Frow, 2006
The Poetics of Prose, Tzvetan Todorov, 1971
The Anatomy of Criticism, Northrop Frye, 1957
Modern Epic, Franco Moretti, 1992
The Trope Thesaurus, Jennifer Hilt, 2021

ABOVE: Jacket cover for Metropolis by Thea von Harbou, The Readers Library Publishing Company Ltd., 1927. Design by Aubrey Hammond. PAGE VI. Jacket cover for Pride and Prejudice, by Jane Austin, George Allen, 1894, Design by Hugh Thomson.

Introduction	1
Early Forms	2
Genre & Medium	4
Trope	6
Theme, Motif, & Symbol	8
Literary Fiction: Novels of Manners	10
Realists & Realism	12
Bildungsroman & Coming of Age	14
Roman à Clef, Autofiction, & Faction	16
Historical Fiction	18
Pastoral & Zeitgeist	20
Imaginative/Speculative Fiction: Gothic & Horror	22
Utopia & Dystopia	24
Science Fiction	26
Fantasy	28
Magical Realism	30
Dramatic / Tonal Fiction: Western & Grit Lit	32
Comedy	34
Satire & Picaresque	36
Love Stories & Romance	38
Suspense Fiction: The Thriller	40
Crime Fiction	42
Detective Fiction & Murder Mystery	44
Young Adult	46
Children's Fiction	48
Non-Fiction: Biography & Memoir	50
Travel & Nature	51
History	52
Current Affairs	53
Popular Science	54
Mind Body Spirit	55
Literary Form: Literary Form	56
Film, TV, & Radio	58

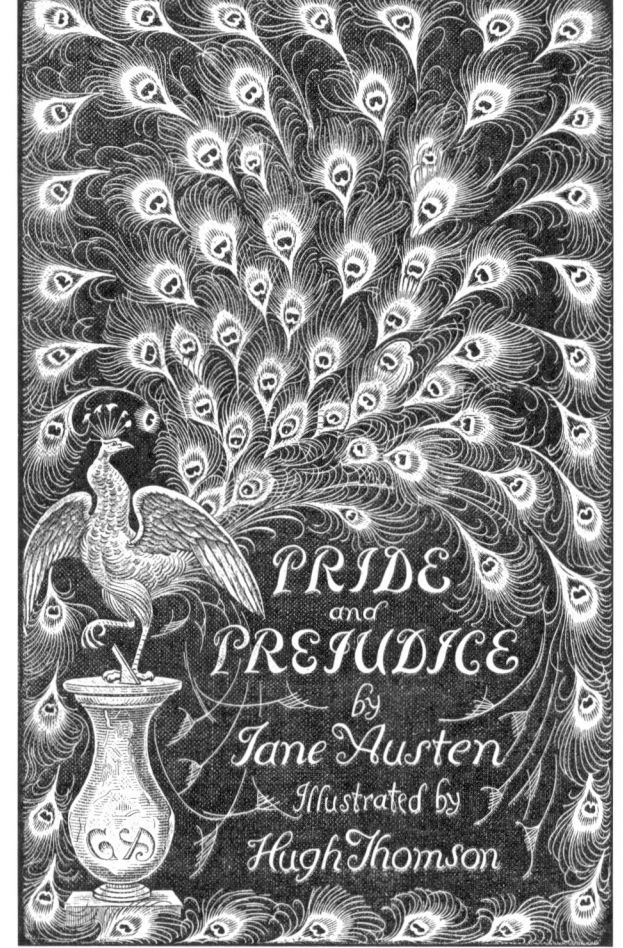

INTRODUCTION

WHY DOES GENRE MATTER and how does it help you as a writer? Any pitch for storytelling, be it novel, film, stage, or radio, will require you to define your work by genre. This gives your audience an insight into what to expect from your piece. Certain genres go through phases of popularity. Agents and publishers were all signing horror fiction in the 1970s and 1980s, and romance and young adult fiction in the 2020s.

The aim of this book is to help writers of all mediums to understand what the characteristics of a genre are, so they can achieve success in their writing. As well as definitions and examples, we present tropes common to each genre. This is not a 'checklist' of things to include, but identifiers which might help in the categorisation process and to offer inspiration if you are still developing your work.

New genres emerge within literature from time to time and I always encourage writers to know what is typical, but also to be free enough to play with rules and expectations. This is a guide book, not a rule book.

Compounding genres is perfectly fine, writers do it all the time. However, it is generally wise to blend no more than two core genres in the description of your work, to ensure that your work has a clear sense of identity, and to encourage immediate recognition in your audience.

This book uses the term 'genre' in its broad theoretical sense, but be aware that 'genre fiction' is also a book trade term, denoting works which are written in accessible styles within certain commercial categories—for example 'genre romance'.

Don't worry, all will become clear over the pages which follow!

EARLY FORMS
the origins of genre

STORYTELLING is an ancient art, but when and why did stories start to be *classified*? In Europe, the mode and purpose of story began to be defined by the ancient Greeks, who categorised their own artistic FORMS as:

EPIC POETRY: Long narrative poems, typically in dactylic hexameter, recounting heroic adventures and mythological stories.

LYRIC POETRY: Personal, often musical verse, expressing emotions, delivered by a single voice (as opposed to a chorus). It included various sub-categories like elegies, epigrams, and odes.

DRAMATIC POETRY (DRAMA): Verse performed by actors taking on roles, divided into: TRAGEDY: Serious dramas exploring human suffering and moral dilemma. COMEDY: Humorous works, often with satire.

SATYR PLAYS: Bawdy entertainment with mythological elements.

PROSE WRITING: Primarily for historical works, dialogues, and rhetorical speeches, not what we would consider 'literature.'

These divisions, especially between tragedy and comedy, represent the emergence of GENRE—distinct categories of storytelling, each with their own rules and conventions. These forms were embedded within specific contexts—religious festivals, civic ceremonies, symposia—that reinforced their principal functions. The audience knew exactly what to expect, emotionally and intellectually, from each genre.

COMEDY and SATYR both permitted a level of social or political critique. Communal laughter is after all intrinsically a good thing— *Homo Ridus* ('laughter is human') says Aristotle. Later writers, like Michel de Montaigne, add that *Homo Risibilus*, 'man is a laughable thing' (*see p.34*).

TRAGEDY, says Aristotle in his *Poetics*, should effect *through pity and fear* an emotional purging, or CATHARSIS. To achieve this a protagonist should possess HAMARTIA (a fatal flaw, misstep, or error), HUBRIS (excessive pride) and EUTYCHĒS (high social status). The UNITY of *time, place, and action* ensure events unfold quickly, in one location, ramping up TENSION, with PERIPETIA (a reversal of fortune) and ANAGNORISIS (a tragic realization) completing the mix. Bloody scenes were kept off the Greek stage, and left to audience imagination; Roman writers would later adore their gore.

THE EPIC mode builds national myth and archetype (the earliest example is the c.2000 BC Sumerian *Epic of Gilgamesh*). Key themes include WANDERING and HOMECOMING. The central character is often a HERO, Odysseus in Homer's 700 BC *Odyssey*, or 5th century Beowulf, or warrior-woman Delhemma in the 11th century Arabic *Sirat Dhat al-Himma*. They are put through a series of increasingly challenging tests, often across a whole lifetime or lifetimes, over vast geographical distances. Temptation, love interests, and otherworldly forces feature strongly.

TRAGIC TROPES include: *The Great But Flawed Noble; Reversal of Fortune; Sudden Loss; Divine Punishment; Fatal Choice; Already Dead; Family Curses; Hubris; Betrayal; Forbidden Love; The Almost; Downfall.* EPIC TROPES include: *Hero of National Importance; Divine Intervention* (Gods get involved); *The Quest; The Epic Journey; Descent to the Underworld; The Secret Heir; Magical Artifact; Fierce Battles; Council of the Elders; Prophecies & Omens; Overcoming Monsters; Superhuman Strength.*

GENRE & MEDIUM
laughter, fears, thrills, tears

Although GENRE today is primarily understood as the style which underpins a work (e.g. Bram Stoker's *Dracula* is GOTHIC) most works are not so easy to categorise, reflecting Jacques Derrida's observation *that participation never amounts to belonging*. Instead, genres overlap and merge into hundreds of subgenres, like HISTORICAL THRILLER, or SCI-FI ROMANCE, alongside constantly emerging hybrids like CYBERPUNK.

This reflects broader cultural shifts toward complexity and the rejection of rigid categories. Ahead of his time, Shakespeare satirises this tendency, probably self-referentially, in *Hamlet*:

> … *tragedy, comedy, history, pastoral, pastoral-comical, historical-pastoral, tragical-historical, tragical-comical-historical-pastoral, scene individable, or poem unlimited*… William Shakespeare, *Hamlet*, Polonius, Act 2, scene 2, lines 383-610.

SUBVERSION and ADAPTION of genre-specific norms are part of any good writer's toolkit. Shakespeare artfully merges all Greek poetic forms into his 'comedies' and 'tragedies'. Arthur Miller's 1949 *Death of a Salesman* inverts the Greek 'hero'—the tragedy of protagonist Willie Loman is not related to his high status or heroic deeds but his pitiful *insignificance*.

The epic mode (*see page 3*) continues to evolve. *War and Peace*, the *Star Wars* films, and *Lord of The Rings* all draw heavily on EPIC STYLE, with their interwoven storylines from different historical periods and dynamic representations of time and space, and EPIC SUBJECT MATTER, the pretext for the action being broader historical myths or events. Writers such as Madeline Miller place often overlooked female characters from ancient works into reimagined epic narratives, e.g in her 2018 novel *Circe*.

Function and genre expectations cross many formats, yet the specific MEDIUM chosen remains a crucial consideration in creative work:

POETRY still excels at LYRIC EXPRESSION. Sonic qualities and metaphorical density create resonances impossible in other forms.

PROSE uniquely enables PSYCHOLOGICAL REALISM, allowing readers direct access to characters' interior lives.

STAGE DRAMA is the natural home for SOCIAL COMEDY, where the shared experience amplifies the recognition of societal absurdities.

RADIO DRAMA creates the perfect conditions for UTOPIAN and DYSTOPIAN fiction, the voice acting and sound effects feeding the imagination.

FILM particularly excels at VISUAL EPIC, using cinematography, editing, and scale to convey sweeping historical narratives.

SERIES TELEVISION offers unparalleled capacity for CHARACTER DRAMA.

VIDEO GAMES create uniquely INTERACTIVE FICTION.

COMICS/GRAPHIC NOVELS are suited to SEQUENTIAL SURREALISM.

EPOQUES and ARTISTIC MOVEMENTS intersect with, and inform, genre. Remember, you are writing in an age yet to be defined, so whatever genre you choose will reflect both this uncertainty and your own intimate connection with the here and now.

TROPE
haven't we met before?

In contemporary literary analysis **TROPES** refer to narrative conventions, character types, and other elements that *recur* across texts and genres (*see opposite*). Cultural theorists like Paul de Man and Kenneth Burke describe tropes as fundamental structures of language and meaning-making, shaping how we understand and communicate ideas in the real world. Although how we define 'real', and how our own narratives bleed into and out of fiction is another story.

Other uses of the word periodically drift into the intellectual zeitgeist, indicating anything with hidden or symbolic meaning, the ultimate shapeshifter for erudite label seekers. Trope is easily confused with **TOPOS** (*Gk* 'place' or 'commonplace') relating to quotidian themes or arguments, originating, like trope, in classical Greek rhetoric.

TV Tropes is one of many online resources that catalogue tropes across all mediums. Essayist Linda Börzsei calls the website:

> *…a technological continuum of classical archetypal literary criticisms, capable of deconstructing recurring elements from creative works in an ironic fashion.*

Media Studies professor Jason Mittell has examined how such trope archiving allows creators to consciously work *with* or *against* established patterns. And this begs the question, are tropes aids or impediments to creativity? As ever, you the writer can figure that one out.

Sometimes a trope may stray into the realms of its *evil twin brother* **CLICHÉ**; or feel *too* ironic, as with any work that includes a Reluctant Chosen One, an Unnecessary Romance, or a Fake-Out Death. Much depends on how they are phrased. The main types of trope are:

GENRE TROPES help define and distinguish particular genres; e.g. in FILM NOIR (genre), the *Femme Fatale* (trope) helps establish atmosphere and theme; *Star-crossed-lovers* are a staple in ROMANTIC TRAGEDY (*below*).

PLOT TROPES are recurring patterns in how stories are structured. These can include PLOT DEVICES like *Chekhov's Gun*, types of STORY ARCS like the *The Fall from Grace*, or BEAT POINTS like the *Secret Identity Reveal*.

CHARACTER TROPES are familiar traits, behaviours, or roles. They are more flexible than a STOCK CHARACTER, not so abstract as ARCHETYPE, and need not be a limit on characterisation. For example, the *Broken Ace* (a competent character with deep personal flaws) can be written in countless ways across multiple genres.

SETTING TROPES involve recurring patterns in how fictional worlds are constructed and presented; e.g. *The City that never sleeps* or *Abandoned Funfair* evoke specific narrative possibilities *and* constraints.

DIALOGUE TROPES are common patterns in how speech and interaction are constructed, e.g. the *Pre-Mortem One-Liner* or *The Cryptic Conversation*.

META TROPES are tropes *about* tropes. *Dead Horse Trope* is a clichéd trope, while *Lampshade Hanging*, where characters explicitly point out a trope, is another way to BREAK THE FOURTH WALL (to acknowledge the fiction of a story).

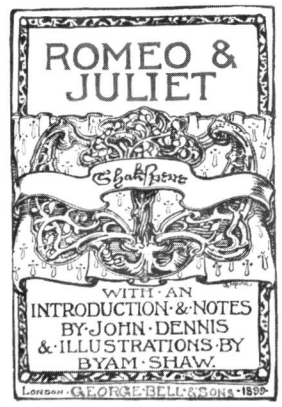

Once you start drilling into trope world, it can be hard to know when to stop, and for some writers the advice is don't even start: *It's turtles all the way down.*

Theme, Motif, & Symbol
all working together

THEME is usually an abstract idea which runs through a work, e.g. 'jealousy' or 'ambition', the central meaning and underlying concern. While genres may have intrinsic concerns (romance explores love, crime fiction examines justice), themes generally transcend genre boundaries.

How themes occur, are perceived, understood, and interpreted are hotly debated subjects. Some writers, like Henry James, contend that extracting message from content is like trying *to separate a smile from a face*. In literary analysis, themes, like tropes, exist on many interconnected levels:

SURFACE: directly addressed through plot (e.g. *love, death*).
PERSONAL: explored through character psychology (e.g. *good vs evil*).
STRUCTURAL: expressed via narrative patterns and organization.
SYMBOLIC: conveyed through imagery (see *motif* and *symbol*).
SOCIAL/HISTORICAL: reflected through cultural context, e.g. *patriarchy*.
PHILOSOPHICAL: explored through the existential or conceptual.
INTER-TEXTUAL: explored in relation to other texts.

A **MOTIF** is a recurring element (image, sound, action, idea, or object) that appears throughout a work, developing symbolic resonance or thematic meaning through repetition and variation. For example, looming shadows in *The Lord of The Rings*, or birds in Charlotte Brontë's works.

SYMBOLS are specific metaphorical elements that represent a larger abstract concept or idea (like a dove symbolising peace). The *crown* in *Macbeth* represents the abstract allure of authority, the *white whale* in *Moby-Dick* symbolises *the unattainable* or God. Boundaries between motif and symbol are often blurred, interacting with theme and trope.

Virginia Woolf's 1925 *Mrs. Dalloway* employs a structural trope of **A day in the life** developed through motifs like flowers (purchased, arranged, worn, and remembered), and Big Ben striking the hours. The waves at the seaside symbolise the eternal cycle of life; Septimus Smith the war-damaged masculine counterpart to Clarissa's domestic confinement. All support themes around individual consciousness and societal constraints.

F. Scott Fitzgerald's 1925 *The Great Gatsby* uses a narrative trope of **The self-made man with a secret past**, developed through motifs like the colour gold and lavish, desperate parties. Faded billboard eyes symbolise abandoned divine judgment. All support themes about the corruption of the American Dream and the hollowness of wealth without authentic connection.

Bram Stoker's 1897 *Dracula* centres on an overarching narrative trope of **The foreign invader threatening civilisation**. To categorise it more fully: *Dracula* takes the *form* of novel; the *genre* is Gothic; its *themes* are identity, gender roles, collaboration, and corruption; its *motifs* are blood, bats, crumbling castles, and violated thresholds (these are also *tropes* as they are repeated throughout the Gothic or horror genre); the motif of blood *symbolises* Victorian fears of miscegenation (among other things), linked to British identity; the creepy abode symbolises aristocratic decay (in other works it could be an eerie suburban mansion, or isolated cabin). Themes of identity, reverse colonisation, and scientific progress were notable Victorian anxieties.

Precise terminology can be a strait-jacket. In this book we use the term 'trope' to refer to *any* feature of a genre which is typical, including recurring motifs, symbols, character types, and plot structures.

NOVELS OF MANNERS
marriage, scandal, trauma

NOVELS OF MANNERS traditionally unfold within the values, rituals, and beliefs of a prosperous, hierarchal society. They both uphold and question class norms and rituals. With tongue slightly in-cheek, mimicking gossipy societal voices, Francis Burney sums up the spirit of the genre:

> *Unused to the situations in which I find myself, and embarrassed by the slightest difficulties, I seldom discover, till too late, how I ought to act.* Frances Burney, Evelina

Jane Austen's 1813 *Pride and Prejudice,* William Thackeray's 1848 *Vanity Fair* and Edith Wharton's 1920 *The Age of Innocence* all adopt similar tones. Protagonists navigate rigid etiquette, working out which norms to stick to, which to resist *and then* stick to (usually marriage), and which they can reject. New works are still written in the genre, especially for screen.

MODERN NOVELS OF MANNERS can be seen in works like Richard Yates' 1961 *Revolutionary Road*, where protagonists struggle with the conformity of suburban living, critiquing and embodying the American Dream:

> *Daddy's a great man because he makes a living, Mummy's a great woman because she's stuck by Daddy all these years — and if old reality ever does pop out and say Boo we'll all get busy and pretend it never happened.*

Other works which focus on how characters navigate subtle cultural expectations while facing modern moral dilemmas include Zadie Smith's 2005 *On Beauty* and Sally Rooney's 2018 *Normal People.* More broadly:

> *What we now call 'literary fiction' is often just the novel of manners in modern dress — it's still about the subtle negotiations of relationships within the constraints of a particular social world.* Claire Messud.

A COMEDY OF MANNERS overtly mocks or caricatures a (usually) upper class paradigm (*see also page 36*). The lampooning is relatively lighthearted, like a youngster teasing an older sibling. P.G. Wodehouse's *Jeeves* novels and Oscar Wilde's plays are brilliantly executed exemplars. Here is Lady Bracknell from *The Importance of Being Earnest* in full flow:

> *To be born, or at any rate bred, in a hand-bag, whether it had handles or not, seems to me to display a contempt for the ordinary decencies of family life that reminds one of the worst excesses of the French Revolution.* Oscar Wilde, 1895.

NOVELS OF MANNERS TROPES include: Marriage (for better, for worse); Imposing Matriarchs with Restrictive Values; Successful Entry into Civilised Society; Gossip; The Regrettable Faux-pas; The Drawing Room Conversation; Social Embarrassment (part of the protagonist's learning curve); Temptations; Rakes (who don't care about their victims' Reputations), later Sacrificed at the Altar of their Folly; Letters And Other Missives, containing the Fates, Hopes, and Fears of characters, Revealing Truths and Making or Breaking Reputations.

REALISTS & REALISM
familiar stories

REALIST writing, which is not genre-specific, captures the essence of *real* life, which, as we know, is complex and nuanced. Equally, as British comedy duo *Mitchell and Webb* point out, *sometimes fires go out, and a cough is just a cough*. Realist writers therefore attempt to represent subject-matter truthfully, while aware that:

> Life is not a series of gig lamps symmetrically arranged; life is a luminous halo, a semi-transparent envelope surrounding us from the beginning of consciousness to the end. Virginia Woolf, critiquing certain aspects of Realism.

REALISM as a literary movement can be contrasted with **ROMANTICISM**. Early works like Flaubert's 1856 *Madame Bovary*, Eliot's 1871 *Middlemarch*, and Tolstoy's 1878 *Anna Karenina* depict ordinary people and contemporary social conditions with unvarnished accuracy. This **SOCIAL REALISM** underpins later novels by Charles Dickens and others, which expose the realities of working class living. Films such as Ken Loach's 1969 *Kes* or 2016 *I, Daniel Blake* or are notable modern examples.

REGIONAL REALISM portrays the reality of a certain place, often a rural or small town community. E. Annie Proulx's 1993 *The Shipping News* captures the harsh environment and unique dialect of Newfoundland. Mark Twain, Thomas Hardy, and John Steinbeck are all celebrated exponents. An evocative matter-of-fact style is the genre's hallmark:

> The Salinas was only a part-time river. The summer sun drove it underground. It was not a fine river at all, but it was the only one we had and so we boasted about it — how dangerous it was in a wet winter and how dry it was in a dry summer.
>
> Steinbeck, *East of Eden*, 1952.

CULTURAL REALISM documents subcultures through their distinctive language, fashion, music, and social ritual. Colin MacInnes' 1959 *Absolute Beginners* follows a teenage photographer through the London jazz scene, interfacing with modernism, race relations, and generational conflict.

PSYCHOLOGICAL REALISM captures the reality of the human mind, our 'inner lives'. The novels of Fyodor Dostoevsky focus intensely on his characters' inner mental and spiritual states. Here is J.G. Ballard in 1974:

> We live in a world ruled by fictions of every kind — mass-merchandising, advertising, politics… We live inside an enormous novel. For the writer in particular it is less and less necessary for him to invent the fictional content of his novel. The fiction is already there. The writer's task is to invent the reality…

THEATRICAL REALISM applies realist principles to drama. The revolutionary NATURALISM of Ibsen's 1879 *A Doll's House* swaps poetic flourishes for natural conversation that reveals character psychology. It confronts contemporary social issues without idealisation or melodrama.

REALISM TROPES: SOCIAL: Working-Class Hero; Kitchen Sink Drama; Strike Episode; Solidarity Forever; The 'Man'; Bath-time. REGIONAL: The Old Homestead; Small Town Boredom; Regional Patriarch/Matriarch; City Mouse vs Country Mouse; The General Store. CULTURAL: Culture Clash; Generation Gap; Food as a Cultural Signifier; The Old Country Flashback; The Cultural Interpreter. PSYCHOLOGICAL: The Unreliable Narrator; Inner Monologue Outer Dialogue Disconnect; Flashback; The Neverending Internal Therapy Session; Mundane Epiphanies.

BILDUNGSROMAN
cradle to grave

A **BILDUNGSROMAN** ('forming novel') offers a chronological overview of a protagonist's life from youth to adulthood, their mistakes, milestones, successes, and failures, along the treacherous path to maturity. Examples include Charlotte Brontë's 1847 *Jane Eyre* and Dickens' 1850 *David Copperfield*.

> Nature made me happy and good, and if I am otherwise, it is society's fault.
>
> Jean-Jacques Rousseau, Emile, 1762.

Goethe's 1795 *Wilhelm Meister's Apprenticeship* is often considered the prototypical bildungsroman, following Wilhelm's journey from bourgeois constraints toward artistic and personal fulfillment, with particular emphasis on philosophical development. Notable 21st century examples include the *Harry Potter* series and Richard Linklater's groundbreaking film *Boyhood*. Many works, like Douglas Stuart's 2020 Booker Prize winner *Shuggie Bain*, further adapt the formula.

BILDUNGSROMAN TROPES include: The Orphan's Journey; The Mentor Who Fails; The School System Rebellion; The Provincial Escape; First Love's Lesson; The False Friend Revelation; The Family Secret Uncovered; The Art vs. Commerce Struggle; The Social Class Awakening; The Awkward Sexual Awakening; First Job Disillusionment; Return Home Changed; The Friend's Tragic Fate; The Financial Reality Check; The Epic Self-Recognition Moment; The Formative Mistake.

COMING OF AGE
change & realisation

A 'COMING OF AGE' novel is a slightly more nuanced bildungsroman, dispensing with the cradle-to-adulthood structure and focusing on a period of self-realisation. Such turning points in life can be tough. In Sylvia Plath's 1963 *The Bell Jar*, protagonist Esther Greenwood uses a fig tree metaphor to describe paralysis in the face of too many possibilities:

> *I saw my life branching out before me like the green fig tree in the story. From the tip of every branch, like a fat purple fig, a wonderful future beckoned and winked…I saw myself sitting in the crotch of this fig tree, starving to death, just because I couldn't make up my mind which of the figs I would choose…*

Teenagers wrestle with who they are, and who they will be, so the genre is especially suited to their stories (*see page 46*). However, we are all changing and evolving, and *The Graduate*, *Stand By Me*, *Clueless* (adapted from Austen's *Emma*), *Dead Poets Society* appeal to all ages.

The genre can be especially poignant if the protagonist's realisation comes well into adulthood. Kazuo Ishiguro's 1989 *The Remains of the Day*, brilliantly adapted for screen in 1993, centres on Stevens, a middle-aged butler who confronts blind loyalty to his former employer, who:

> *… chose a certain path in life, it proved to be a misguided one, but there, he chose it, he can say that at least. As for myself, I cannot even claim that.*

COMING OF AGE TROPES include: *The 'Talk'; Heroes are flawed; The Road Trip; The Journey; The Life Crisis Catalyst; The Road Not Taken; The Empty Nest; Reluctant Return Home; The Family Crisis; Teenage Rebellion; The Party; Mid-life Rebellion; Grief as Transformation; The Second Chance at Love.*

ROMAN À CLEF
likely stories

The **ROMAN À CLEF** ('novel with a key') depicts real people and events under different names. This allows for narrative freedom and, as described by critic John Mullan, *a sense of revealing what has been secret, of broaching the forbidden*. It is not always obvious that you are reading a roman à clef. Orwell's *Animal Farm* stands alone as allegory but is also a critique of the Russian revolution. William Amos' *The Originals: Who's Really Who In Fiction* unearths these hidden layers.

A roman à clef is a good vehicle for: **COMEDY** (Monty Python's *The Life of Brian*); **REVENGE** (Lady Caroline Lamb's *Glenarvon,* exposing Lord Byron's treatment of her); **AVOIDING DEFAMATION** (Joe Klein's *Primary Colours*); and **POLITICAL SATIRE** (Richard Condon's *The Manchurian Candidate*).

The Coen brothers chose to make the *Fargo* series into a faux 'Série à Clef' adding one of their trademark disclaimers:

> This is a true story. The events depicted in this film took place in Minnesota in 1987. At the request of the survivors, the names have been changed. Out of respect for the dead, the rest has been told exactly as it occurred.

ROMAN À CLEF TROPES include: *The Thinly Disguised Celebrity Takedown; The "All Resemblance to Persons Living or Dead is Purely Coincidental" Wink; The Industry Exposé Nobody Asked For; The Academic Backstabbing Chronicle; The "This Definitely Isn't My Ex" Character; The Revenge of the Ex* (400 pages to process what therapy couldn't fix); *The Hollywood Tell-Most* (reveals everything except the stuff that gets you blacklisted); *The Double Bluff* (the true subject, who has a different name, appears in the book as a 'different' character, under their real name); *Insider Perspective* (narration from someone with special access).

AUTOFICTION & FACTION
couldn't make it up

FICTIONAL BIOGRAPHY is an immersive form of biographical narrative which adds imagined scenes and dialogue. **AUTOFICTION** does the same from a first-person perspective. Both are intentionally stylised works which turn real life into a novel, deliberately blurring the boundaries between reality and invention, removing the shackles of accuracy:

> In place of numerous foster homes in which the child Norma Jean lived, 'Blonde' explores only one and that fictitious; in place of numerous lovers, medical crises, abortions and suicide attempts and screen performances, 'Blonde' explores only a select, symbolic few. Joyce Carol Oates, Blonde, author's note.

TRUE FICTION (FACTION), such as Tom Wolfe's 1979 *The Right Stuff* takes greater liberties with fact. Still based on real events, it more freely adds fictional elements to serve the narrative. **NON-FICTION NOVELS** combine journalistic research and factual reporting; an **The Immersive Deep Dive** with the visceral power of a novel (*see also Crime Fiction p. 42*).

AUTOFICTION TROPES include: **The Family History Investigation**; **The Multiple Version Event**; **The Intimate Revelation Regret**; **The Childhood Memory Revision**; **Metafictional Commentary** like **The Creative Process Mirror** where writing the book becomes a central theme within the book itself. **TRUEFICTION TROPES**: **Composite Character Creation** (multiple real people condensed into one fictional representative); **The Authentic False Document** (letters, journals, or reports mimicking historical artifacts). **NON-FICTION NOVEL TROPES**: **The Temporal Compression** (years of events artfully condensed into representative scenes and moments); **The Recursive Interview** (subjects' testimonies integrated into the story while acknowledging the interview process itself).

HISTORICAL FICTION
reliving past lives

HISTORICAL FICTION, writes Sarah Johnson of the *Historical Novels Review Journal*, is set fifty or more years in the past, and written principally from research rather than personal experience. A work of historical fiction (film or prose) can adopt one of three broad approaches:

INVENTED CHARACTERS, IN A REAL PAST. Fictional protagonists within meticulously drawn historical settings. Sir Walter Scott arguably invented the genre with his 1814 *Waverley* (set in 1745 Scotland) and 1819 *Ivanhoe* (12th century England). Others soon followed, e.g. Dickens' 1859 *A Tale of Two Cities* (London and Paris 1790s), Tolstoy's 1867 *War and Peace* (Russia between 1805 and 1820). An excellent recent example is Vikram Seth's 1993 *A Suitable Boy* (post-independence India).

REAL CHARACTERS, IN A REAL PAST. A reimagined history, grounded in historical reality, but with maximum narrative freedom. Tracy Chevalier's 1999 *Girl with a Pearl Earring* (17th century Delft) imagines a relationship between Vermeer and his model. Maggie O'Farrell's 2020 *Hamnet* explores Shakespeare's family life and the death of his son.

ALTERNATE HISTORY asks 'what if?' Jillian Cantor's 2021 *Half Life* reimagines Marie Curie's life had she made different choices. Kim Stanley Robinson's 2002 *The Years of Rice and Salt* imagines world development if the Black Death had wiped out 99% of Europe's population. Philip K. Dick's 1962 *The Man in the High Castle* depicts an America where the Axis powers won World War II.

Some writers invent a fictional protagonist to tell the story of a historical character. In Robert Harris's *Cicero Trilogy*, the protagonist is not actually Marcus Tullius Cicero himself, but rather his secretary, Tiro. Historical lives can also be depicted with minimal invention, adopting a more factional approach (*see page 17*), e.g. Irving Stone's 1961 *The Agony and the Ecstasy* about Michelangelo. Hilary Mantel's 1992 *A Place of Greater Safety* (French Revolution) and 2009 *Wolf Hall* (Tudor England) are exemplars of the modern genre. Her advice is to:

> Know ten times as much as you tell. When you not only know what your characters wore, but you can feel their clothes on your back: that rasp of homespun wool: that whisper of linen and weight of brocade. When you can answer these questions, you are ready to begin. 2017 Reith Lectures Resurrection: The Art and Craft

Subgenres include TIME-SLIP NOVELS, where characters travel between contemporary and historical settings, as in Diana Gabaldon's *Outlander* series. In Virginia Wolf's 1928 *Orlando*, the eponymous protagonist experiences time linearly but at an abnormal pace—neither time slip nor time travel—living through centuries of British history and literary movements. HISTORICAL MYSTERIES, such as C.J. Sansom's *Shardlake* series, set detective stories in past eras.

HISTORICAL FICTION TROPES include: The Witness to History (all through the eyes of an ordinary Joe); The Conveniently Modern Protagonist; Exposition Through Servant Gossip; The Rise and Fall Arc; The Overly-Researched Meal Scene; The Betrayal; The Plague That Spares The Main Characters; The Progressive Love Interest; Corrupt Clergy; Vaguely Accurate Slang; The Improbably Literate Commoner; The Background War (never seen); The Corset Complaint (restrictive undergarments); The Innovative Viewpoint.

Pastoral
shepherd's delight

Pastoral works, from the Latin *pastor* ('shepherd'), evoke the Rural Idyll. The genre has very ancient roots which connect to our pre-agricultural past. In Greek and Roman literature The Shepherd is a staple, very often surrounded by mythical nymphs and dryads, embodying a Golden Age of rustic innocence and peace (*see page i*), an *Arcadia* where:

> *The soil will need no harrowing, the vine no pruning knife,*
> *And the tough ploughman may at last unyoke his oxen.* Virgil 1983: 19.

Shakespeare and Renaissance poets also drew on the shepherd motif. In later pastorals, like Hardy's 1874 *Far from the Madding Crowd*, shepherds are no longer required. Country folk and rural landscapes take their place, celebrating a slower pace of life, often with a contemplative tone.

Modern Pastorals probe the realities of modern rural life, or celebrate a 'return to nature', as in Melissa Harrison's 2015 *At Hawthorn Time*, or Annie Dillard's 1974 non-fiction *The Pilgrim at Tinker Creek*:

> *I live by a creek, Tinker Creek, in a valley in Virginia's Blue Ridge. An anchorite's hermitage is called an anchor-hold; some anchor-holds were simple sheds clamped to the side of a church like a barnacle or a rock. I think of this house clamped to the side of Tinker Creek as an anchor-hold.*

> Pastoral Tropes: The Shepherd/Ploughboy/Farmer/Milkmaid (closer to nature than other humans). Mythical Creatures; Rural Isolation; The Land or Landscape (as an emblem for the power and vastness of the Natural World); Floods; Storms; Droughts; Arcadia or a Lost Golden Age; The Urban World is Corrupt and Far Away; Beautiful Maidens and Wholesome Toilers.

ZEITGEIST
dramatising the issue

ZEITGEIST FICTION refers to literature that captures and reflects the defining spirit, mood, issues, and preoccupations of a time in history. Examples include Dostoevsky's *Demons*, Joseph Heller's *Catch-22*, Jay McInerney's *Bright Lights, Big City*, and Sally Rooney's *Normal People*.

A pressing issue of our time is addressed by **ECOFICTION**. Daniel Quinn's 1992 *Ishmael* probes humanity's destructive 'othering' of the natural world. Ernest Callenbach's 1975 *Ecotopia* imagines a society governed on ecological principals within a sustainable economy.

CLIMATE FICTION (CLI-FI) blends scientific understanding with human drama; e.g. Barbara Kingsolver's 2012 *Flight Behavior*.

ENVIRONMENTAL JUSTICE FICTION incorporates indigenous or first nation perspectives; e.g. Amitav Ghosh's 2004 *The Hungry Tide*.

GAIA FICTION features biocentric perspectives; e.g. Richard Powers' 2018 *The Overstory*.

DYSTOPIAN ECO-FICTION imagines the worst. Robert C. O'Brien's 1973 *Z for Zachariah* depicts life in a radiation-poisoned world.

ECO-FICTION TROPES include: The Last Forest Guardian; The Corporate Scientist's Crisis; The Water War; The Seed Bank Quest; The Tree-Time Perspective; The Eco-Terrorist's Dilemma; The Last Species Pair (final chance); The Weather Engineer's Mistake (science gone wrong); Nature's Revenge; The Climate Refugee; Solarpunk Optimism.

GOTHIC & HORROR
scared to death

GOTHIC literature uses atmosphere, suggestion, and psychological unease to evoke **DREAD**, focusing on the sublime tension between terror and beauty within recognizable social frameworks. It plays on the fears of society at a particular time, for what we find scary is always changing.

Gothic elements, e.g. **UNSETTLING ATMOSPHERES**, already appear in Shakespeare (*our Gothic bard*, according to Elizabeth Montague), but the heyday of the genre is the Romantic epoch (c.1780–1850), when it distilled the anxiety of society's transition from rural to industrial life. The first 'pure Gothic' novel is considered to be Walpole's 1764 *The Castle of Otranto*, while Ann Radcliffe's 1794 *The Mysteries of Udolpho* follows a young female protagonist who *almost* falls victim to a range of supernatural threats in an ancient castle. Radcliffe writes about the genre:

> Terror and horror are so far opposite, that the first expands the soul, and awakens the faculties to a high degree of life; the other contracts, freezes, and nearly annihilates them. Ann Radcliffe, On the Supernatural in Poetry, 1826.

HORROR aims to shock and frighten. There tends to be less emphasis on atmospheric buildup or social context, more on explicit violence, gore, and threats. The genre arguably begins with Matthew Lewis' 1796 *The Monk* which corrupted the Gothic form with scenes of rape, murder, and Satanic seduction. For Radcliffe, and exponents like Alfred Hitchcock, such explicit scenes are part of an inferior approach. The genre becomes more codified in the late 19th and early 20th centuries with writers like H.P. Lovecraft and Edgar Allan Poe probing the edges of sanity. Horror is the highest grossing film genre today—a truly terrifying thought.

THE SUPERNATURAL is a mainstay of both Gothic and horror and yet is treated differently by each. In pure Gothic form, mysterious phenomena are often explainable (ghostly clankings turn out to be a prisoner in a hidden chamber), while for Lewis, and later horror writers like Stephen King, the supernatural could be very real, and very violent.

Willing suspension of disbelief also underpins both genres. Past and foreign settings, frame narratives, and extensive use of epistolary are widely used to aid immersion and believability.

GOTHIC TROPES: EARLY: The Revenant; The Past Haunts the Present; Ancient Castles; Medieval Buildings; Empty Churches; Hidden Familial Ties; Predatory Patriarchs; Damsels in Distress; Dubious Foreign Countries. ROMANTIC: The Sublime (original sense); Epiphanies (of the beauty of nature); The Exotic Other; Faustian Bargain. 19TH CENTURY: Cursed Objects; Coffins; Spooky Country Houses; Family Secrets; Locked Rooms; Twisted Trees; Crows and Ravens; Secrets in the Attic. FIN DE SIÈCLE: Doubles and Doppelgängers; The Monster Within. SOUTHERN: Injury/Disability; Incest; Racial Divides; Corrupted Religion; Fallen Grandeur (see Faulkner's A Rose for Emily).

HORROR TROPES: Creepy Children; Lurking Presence; Sudden Violence; Descent Into Madness; Bones; Blood; Guts; Severed Body Parts; Bleeding from Eyes; Power Tools; Possession; Hideous Clues; Unstoppable Killer; Creaky Doors; Maggoty Meat; Giant Spiders; Kiss and You Die; Abandoned Playrooms; Broken Dolls.

UTOPIA & DYSTOPIA
too good to be true or just too bad

UTOPIAS are imagined, idealised worlds which offer solutions to perceived social problems. The term comes from Thomas More's 1516 *Utopia*. More knew that idealised worlds were not necessarily realistic, so 'utopia' originally meant 'no-place'. His island utopia eschewed material wealth, and featured communal living, free lectures, and shared possessions (also slaves and some questionable martial practices).

Though not named as such, we find utopias in ancient Greece and Rome (in Plato's *Republic* and Lucian's *A True History*), and in Christian theology (the Garden of Eden). Many utopias have **ALLEGORY** behind them, but others are just hedonistic and chaotic, such as Cockayne, a fantastic land of plenty which crops up in various medieval European traditions. Cockayne is a place where larks:

> **Land in your mouth, well-cooked and tame, / Freshly stewed and nicely done, / Sprinkled with cloves and cinnamon.** London, British Library, MS Harley 913, ff. 3r-6v

DYSTOPIAS are instead products of **ZEITGEIST**, often taking a contemporary anxiety and imagining its worst case scenario or most grisly 'solution'. Various subgenres exist, principally:

ENVIRONMENTAL DYSTOPIAS: a change in climate or ecology makes life as we know it impossible, e.g. J. G. Ballard's 1962 *The Drowned World*.

BIOLOGICAL DYSTOPIAS: virus or disease attacks humans or our food systems, e.g. Richard Mathesen's 1954 *I am Legend*.

TECHNOLOGICAL DYSTOPIAS: machines finally take over, e.g. Ray Bradbury's 1950 *There will Come Soft Rains*.

POLITICAL DYSTOPIAS: the state takes over, e.g. George Orwell's 1949 *1984*.

ANTI-UTOPIA is a subgenre of dystopic writing which recognises that one person's utopia is another's dystopia. It poses specific questions, such as: *"What is better, freedom or happiness?"*, *"Should we advocate 'freedom to' or 'freedom from'?"*, and *"Should societies be 'we' based (collective), or 'I' based (individualistic)?"*.

Yevgeny Zamyatin's 1921 *We*, written in response to the Russian revolution, introduced many of the tropes outlined below, as well as directly influencing George Orwell's *1984*, Margaret Atwood's 1985 *The Handmaid's Tale* and Aldous Huxley's 1932 *Brave New World*.

Utopia and Dystopia have always been intrinsically linked—the original definition of paradise is 'a walled enclosure'. Indeed any utopia, if depicted skillfully, will feature challenges yet to be overcome, human failings, and even a dark underbelly.

TROPES COMMON TO BOTH include: **Islands or Walls** to keep citizens 'in' and outsiders 'out'; **Eugenics and State Childrearing**; **Hierarchy**; **Censorship**; **The Primitive** (like John 'the Savage' in Brave New World or Yahoos in Gulliver's Travels); **Atavistic Traits** (like the 'hairy hands' of D503 in We). DYSTOPIAN TROPES: **The Rebellion Catalyst** (often personified as 'Eve like' women awakening male conscience, see Julia in *1984*, D207 in We); **The Overlord or Big Boss** (real or imagined); **The Orwellian Naming Department**—'Ministry of Love' specializing in torture or 'Joy Camps' featuring forced labor; **Drug-Induced Compliance**. UTOPIAN TROPES: **The Benevolent Council of Elders**; **The Uniform Fashion Choice** (nothing says 'perfect society' like everyone dressed identically); **The Eliminated Currency System**; **Knowledge-Transfer-Without-Schools**.

SCIENCE FICTION
the shape of things to come

SCI-FI is set in the future, or far far away, with individuals and societies immersed in or confronting science and technology beyond our own. The secret to its success lies in our imagination, argues Will Storr:

> The brain's propensity for automatic model making is exploited with superb effect by tellers of fantasy and science fiction stories. Simply naming a planet, ancient war or obscure technical detail seems to trigger the neural process of building it, as if it actually exists [...]. In Blade Runner's most famous scene, replicant Roy Batty, on the edge of death, tells Rick Deckard, "I've seen things you wouldn't believe. Attack ships on fire off the shoulder of Orion. I watched C beams glitter in the dark near the Tannhauser gate". Those C beams! That gate! The Science of Storytelling, 2019.

HARD SCIENCE FICTION often reimagines an extreme world, far from the familiar; e.g. Philip K Dick's 1968 *Do Androids Dream of Electric Sheep?*, and attempts scientific accuracy, as in Andy Weir's 2011 *The Martian*.

SOFT SCIENCE FICTION tends towards a more recognisable world, with less newness, as in Kazuo Ishiguro's 2021 *Klara and the Sun*, and less focus on scientific accuracy; e.g. Pierre Boulle's 1963 *Planet of the Apes*.

Iain Banks, one of the genre's most successful writers, famously could not get his hard SF work published until he broke in to the 'literary world' with *The Wasp Factory*, yet he considers SF the most important genre:

> ... one that deals directly with the effects of change, and specifically technological change, on people and society. And that has been one of the most important aspects of our lives since the industrial revolution. [...] mainstream writing touches on it but doesn't concentrate on it. Iain Banks, Interview for Wired Magazine, 2010.

The genre hybridises easily, as **GOTHIC SCI-FI** (*Frankenstein*) or **HORROR SCI-FI**; e.g. Peter Hamilton's 1996 *Reality Dysfunction*. Subgenres include:

ALIEN INVASION: Extraterrestrials come to Earth. Stories can range from outright invasion to more subtle first contact scenarios.

TIME TRAVEL: Characters can move through time in various ways. Explores causality and the consequences of changing historical events.

SPACE OPERA: Epic adventures across vast galactic settings. Sweeping conflicts, advanced civilizations, and interstellar travel; *Star Wars/Dune*.

CYBERPUNK: Set in dystopian futures dominated by megacorporations, AI and virtual reality. Similar to its shiny brass sibling **STEAMPUNK**.

BIOPUNK: Explores biotechnology and its impact on society, including the manipulation of genetic material and living organisms.

POST APOCALYPTIC: Imagines societies after some form of future global catastrophe, man-made or natural. Can be similar to ecofiction (*see page 21*).

SCI-FI TROPES include: *Deadly Aliens* (right); *Inhospitable Landscapes*; *AI Robots*; *Close Confines*; *Spaceships*; *Colonies*; *Outposts*; *Robot Uprising*; *Clones*; *Time Travel*; *Techno-Gibberish* (Hans Solo: "made the Kessel Run in less than 12 parsecs"); *Hive Mind* (*Ender's Game*); *Megastructures*; *Nanotech*; *Robots Like Us*; *Neural Interfaces* (wetware); *Augmented Bodies*; *Insane Weaponry*; *Wormholes Through Spacetime*; *Interspecies Romance*; *Promethean Errors* (new technologies go bad); *Mind Uploads* (*Ghost in the Shell*) and *Downloads*.

FANTASY
the art of the otherworld

FANTASY is described by J.R.R. Tolkien as *the making or glimpsing of Otherworlds*. Fantasy writing, he says, is an *elvish craft* requiring creative *magic*.

HIGH FANTASY describes works such as Mervyn Peake's 1950 *Gormenghast* in which **WORLD-BUILDING** creates entire **SECONDARY WORLDS**. All the action takes place in these coherent secondary realities, with their own physical laws, magical systems, cultural histories, mythologies, and geographies. They are alien enough to evoke wonder, but consistent enough to be believable. To achieve this, Ursula Le Guin, author of the *Earthsea* series, highlights the importance of skillful writing:

> *Exact and vivid words make an exact and vivid world. The fantasy writer must "believe in" the world she is creating — dwelling in it while writing, and trusting it to reveal itself.* Ursula Le Guin, Plausibility in Fantasy, An open letter.

LOW FANTASY works, like Mary Norton's 1952 *The Borrowers*, are set in a **PRIMARY WORLD**, usually one that functions in the same way as our own. Magic and magical objects are more limited in scope, existing in the margins or shadows of society (*see also Magic Realism page 30*).

There are many grades between 'low' and 'high'. Real and imagined worlds can exist alongside one another, connected via a **PORTAL**. In Phillip Pullman's *Northern Lights* trilogy the world is both familiar *and* very different. Fantasy texts tend to lean on the **HERO'S JOURNEY** (see our sister book *Plot*). Here are some more subgenres of this genre:

URBAN FANTASY is set in contemporary cities; often with supernatural creatures living in secret among humans; e.g. J. Butcher's *Dresden Files*.

Dark Fantasy adds elements of horror and explores darker themes with morally ambiguous characters; e.g. Joe Abercrombie's *First Law* series.

Sword and Sorcery focuses on sword-wielding heroes, monsters, and episodic adventures; e.g. Fritz Leiber's *Fafhrd and the Gray Mouser* series.

Historical Fantasy takes place in historical settings or alternate versions of them; e.g. Susanna Clarke's *Jonathan Strange & Mr Norrell*.

Fantasy evolved from epic traditions (*see page 2*), inheriting their heroic quests, supernatural elements, and grand-scale conflicts between good and evil. Unlike epic's claimed historicity, fantasy instead explicitly presents itself as imaginative invention. Works like Tolkien's 1955 *The Lord of the Rings* adopt epic structures and linguistic patterns, fusing them with modern literary techniques and psychological complexity. This hybrid approach continues in contemporary works which mine epic traditions for **Mythic Resonance**.

Fantasy Tropes include: *Big Bads & Dark Overlords*; *Living Architecture*; *Magical Objects*; *Threshold Guardians*; *Forgotten Deities*; *Sympathetic Systems* (objects connected to their targets); *Blood Legacy* (inherited magical abilities); *Soul-Bonded Weapons* (choose their wielders and share their fates); *Mythical Creatures* (dragons/elves/fairies); *Magical Transformations*; *High Calorie Food* (one biscuit per 1350 miles); *Wizard Fashion* (impractical robes and pointy hats); *Magical System Limitations* (spells work perfectly except on Tuesdays); *Guild Systems*; *Animal Helpers*; *The Spell That Backfires*.

MAGICAL REALISM
everyday strange

MAGICAL REALISM integrates irreducible or 'magical' elements into otherwise realistic narratives, blurring the boundaries between the fantastic and the mundane. Focused attempts to pin down its core features seek to avoid the potential for reductive labelling. Professor Wendy B. Faris suggests five core characteristics:

1. The text contains an irreducible ELEMENT OF MAGIC, something we cannot explain according to the laws of the universe as we know them.
2. DESCRIPTION is characterized by a strong emphasis on the physical, observable world, often through extensive and precise detail—this is the 'realism' aspect that distinguishes it from pure fantasy or allegory.
3. The reader may HESITATE (at one point or another) between two contradictory understandings of events, experiencing some unsettling doubts.
4. We experience the closeness or NEAR-MERGING of two realms or worlds.
5. We question received ideas about TIME, SPACE, AND IDENTITY.

The inexplicable 'magical' thing can be anything from: people who talk to cats (Haruki Murakami's 2002 *Kafka on the Shore*); to plagues of insomnia (Gabriel Garcia Marquez's 1967 *One Hundred Years of Solitude*); women who are psychic healers (Toni Morrison's 1997 *Paradise*); and dancers who suddenly finding themselves floating in the sky:

> And she laughed and stamped the ground a little harder and rose a few inches above the pavement, pulling the others along with her, and before long not one of them was touching the ground, they were taking 2 steps in place and one step forward without touching the ground... Kundera, The Book of Laughter and Forgetting, 1978.

Scholar Luis Leal notes that *In magical realism the writer confronts reality and tries to untangle it.* This engagement with, and questioning of, the phenomenal world is born out in various subcategories of the genre, which include colonial, post-colonial, feminist, indigenous, and contemporary urban contexts. Thus, Kundera's disillusionment with the Czech Communist Revolution is deeply reflected in his work; Guillermo del Toro's 2006 film *Pan's Labyrinth* is set against a backdrop of the Spanish Civil War.

MAGIC REALISM (note the capital 'M' and 'R') was an art movement before a literary genre, describing the *Magischer Realismus* of 1920's post-expressionist artists like Otto Dix. Latin America writers in the late 1940s were greatly influenced by the strange dreamlike precision and unsettling clarity of such images, which they then morphed into literary form.

MAGICAL REALISM TROPES include: *Ancestral Visitations; Strange Bodily Manifestations of Emotion; Magical Bloodlines; Nature Responding to Human Events; Objects with Memory; Prophetic Dreams Becoming Reality; Physical Impossibilities Accepted as Routine; Cultural Memory Materializing* (collective traumas/ triumphs appear as tangible phenomena). TROPES MAY MANIFEST AS: *Literal Maternal Omniscience* (mothers with actual eyes in the back of their heads); *The Literally Magnetic Personality* (characters whose emotions cause kitchenware to orbit them in arguments); *The Metaphor That Didn't Get the Memo* (character whose heart literally breaks); *The Emotional Weather System* (feelings manifest as climate events; making first dates particularly hazardous).

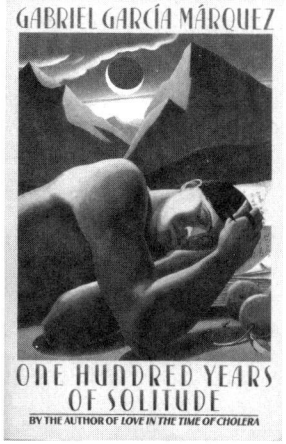

WESTERN
natives and settlers

WESTERNS get their name from the colonial idea of 'Manifest Destiny', that 19th century European 'settlers' had an inalienable right to 'go West and conquer America'. Frank Gruber outlines seven plots for traditional Westerns (1900–1950) which mythologise frontier expansion:

UNION PACIFIC STORY: plotted around railroad, telegraph, or wagon.
RANCH STORY: how to fend off natives, rustlers or large landowners.
EMPIRE STORY: a rags-to-riches tale where we back the capitalist.
REVENGE STORY: a protagonist seeks retribution for a past wrong.
CAVALRY AND NATIVES STORY: 'taming' the frontier.
OUTLAW STORY: Anti-Heros we root for, or Villains we despise.
MARSHAL STORY: a lawman trying to do his duty.

Revisionist variants like SPAGHETTI WESTERNS go some way to challenging these narratives—which systematically erase or caricature indigenous perspectives. *Dances with Wolves* (1990) depicts the destruction of Lakota culture and the broken treaties that facilitated it.

WESTERN TROPES include: The Stranger Riding into Town; Frontier Justice; The Quickdraw Showdown at Noon; The Sharpshooter Who Never Misses; The Town with Exactly One Woman; The Homesteader; Tumbleweed as Dramatic Punctuation; The Sheriff One Day from Retirement (or a coffin); The Saloon Doors That Never Close; The Bandit with a Code of Honour (tips his hat to ladies).

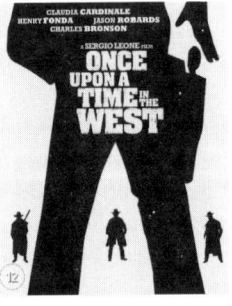

Grit Lit
rugged with a heart

Instead of romanticising frontier life and death, **Grit-Lit** offers raw, unvarnished depictions of working-class and rural people, struggling with poverty, addiction, violence, and limited opportunities.

> The practitioners of Grit Lit have more often than not come from the very landscape they describe; they've fought their way up from the ground ... They were the sensitive guy at the dogfight, the guy who shot the deer even though he'd rather be at home reading. Tom Franklin

Grit Lit heroes, like John Grady Cole in Cormac McCarthy's *All the Pretty Horses*, are competent players in a rough and ready world. The dangers they face give them a hardened exterior but a pensive nature; they exhibit more feeling than any traditional gunslinger might care to admit:

> He picked out the smallest doe among them and shot her.... The sky was dark and a cold wind ran through the bajada and in the dying light [...] Grass and blood. Blood and stone. Cormac McCarthy, All the Pretty Horses, 1992.

Grit Lit Tropes include: The Damaged Protagonist; The Rusty Truck (that never dies); The Family Secret Everyone Knows; Cycles of Violence; The Grandmother Holding Everything Together; Substance Abuse; Failed Escape Attempts (all roads lead back home); The Beloved Dog With One Good Year Left; DIY Justice; The Factory That's Always Closing; Broken Families; The Prison Stint Everyone Saw Coming (bad decisions made official); Peculiar Codes of Honour; The Hunting Trip as Therapy; Economic Desperation; The Temporary Trailer (15 years now); The Local Bar Tab as Economic Indicator; The Family Bible With Sporadic Use (dusted off for weddings, funerals, and emergencies).

COMEDY
the best medicine

COMEDY taps into our innate desire to laugh, while reminding us that we ourselves are ridiculous. In pointing this out, comedy writers risk giving offense, so they generally require very thick skins:

> *What we find funny is subjective. A good rule of thumb is that if you're chuckling to yourself as you write, the chances are that at least some other people will laugh when they read what you've written. But you can be certain that for every person laughing there will be someone else rolling their eyes and tutting.*
>
> Maria Lewycka, author of A Short History of Tractors in Ukrainian

Comedy is often said to revolve around SITUATION (the basic setup, misunderstandings and all), STYLE (choice of language and comedic techniques), and TIMING (the rhythm of delivery, punchlines, and pauses). Building and subverting expectations, often using tropes, is also key: *Introduce-Reinforce-Subvert*. *The most familiar joke is when we expect one thing, but something else is said*, writes Cicero in *De Oratore* c. 55 BC, a sentiment echoed nearly two millennia later by English essayist William Hazlitt:

> *The essence of the laughable then is the incongruous, the disconnecting one idea from another, or the jostling of one feeling against another.*

Some comedic forms, like the exaggerated physical mishaps of SLAPSTICK, primarily work visually. Others, like the short format, standalone scenes of SKETCH COMEDY are best suited for stage, screen, and audio formats. Here are some of the main subgenres of comedy:

FARCE employs exaggerated situations, physical humour, and improbable coincidences, e.g. Oscar Wilde's 1895 *The Importance of Being Earnest*.

COMIC FANTASY & SCI-FI employs absurd speculative scenarios, often parodying genre conventions; e.g. *The Hitchhiker's Guide to the Galaxy* by Douglas Adams and *Discworld* series by Terry Pratchett.

ROMANTIC COMEDY centres on romantic entanglements and misunderstandings; e.g. Shakespeare's *Much Ado About Nothing*, films like *Love Actually*, and more nuanced novels like Andrew Sean Greer's 2017 *Less*.

BLACK COMEDY takes on serious, disturbing, or taboo subjects; e.g. Bret Easton Ellis' *American Psycho*, and *Slaughterhouse-Five* by Kurt Vonnegut.

ABSURDIST COMEDY employs illogical situations, nonsensical elements, and non-sequiturs. Franz Kafka is a seminal exponent.

CAMPUS COMEDY satirizes academic life and intellectual pretensions; e.g. *Lucky Jim* by Kingsley Amis or *Straight Man* by Richard Russo.

COMEDY TROPES include: The Falling Object Dodged; Disproportionate Reactions (small things become crises); Fish out of Water; Straight Man & Stooge; Dramatic Irony (we know stuff they don't); The Un-Average Protagonist (ordinary character with suspiciously good looks, apartment, and wit); The Incompetent Authority Figure; The Well-Timed Medical Emergency; It's Funny 'cos it's True; It's Funny 'cos he's an Idiot; Normal Activity Done Wrong (making tea by screaming at water); The Reveal; The Workplace Where No Work Happens (romance); Mistaken Identity; Rain-Soaked Declaration of Love (pneumonia as commitment); Competitive Grief; Comedic Misunderstanding (characters talk past each other); Role Reversal; Cause Bizarre Effect (actions lead to unexpected consequences); Aliens Obsessed With Trivia (e.g. paper clips); Repetition with Escalation.

SATIRE
the sharpest weapon

SATIRE, a grown up and sophisticated scion of comedy, acts as a hall of mirrors to society: slight distortions of reality emphasise existing flaws. The genre has roots at least as far back as ancient Greece.

MENIPPEAN SATIRE attacks attitudes and dogmas rather than individuals and is characterized by a mix of styles and viewpoints; e.g. Swift's 1704 *A Tale of a Tub* mocks religious excesses; Thomas Carlyle's 1834 *Sartor Resartus* centres on a fictional philosopher's absurd theories.

HORATIAN SATIRE uses gentle, witty, and humorous criticism of human folly and social conventions, aiming to correct through humour and clever observations. Jane Austen's 1813 *Pride and Prejudice* is a classic example, as is Alexander Pope's 1712 *The Rape of the Lock* with its mock-heroic treatment of trivial social incidents.

JUVENALIAN SATIRE is darker, more contemptuous and indignant, often expressing moral outrage through savage criticism; e.g. Orwell's 1945 *Animal Farm*, or Swift's 1729 *A Modest Proposal* which suggested eating children to solve poverty.

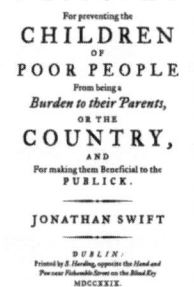

SATIRICAL TROPES: *Hyperbole as Unveiling* (exaggeration); *Ironic Juxtaposition* (contradictory elements highlight hypocrisy); *Satiric Persona* (character whose biases become the mechanism for criticism); *Reductio ad Absurdum* (e.g. Capitalism evolving until oxygen requires a subscription); *Role Reversal*; *Allegory*; *Mock Heroic Treatment* (e.g. praise of fleas).

PICARESQUE
shaggy dogs

THE PICARESQUE novel follows a Rogue Who Fails Upward, an endearing protagonist (a *pícaro*) of low social status who survives a series of misadventures though wit, cunning, charm or sheer fluke. These (usually) episodic tales, mostly told from the protagonist's viewpoint, combine social satire with comedy, exposing society's hypocrisies and corruptions.

> Don't think too hard about this stuff for the time being. Just go with the flow. Things like this don't happen all that often in one lifetime. This is the magnificent world of a picaresque novel. Just brace yourself and enjoy the smell of evil. We're shooting the rapids. And when we go over the falls, let's do it together in grand style. Haruki Murakami, 1Q84, 2009

Picaro stories range from the medieval *Reynard the Fox*, Daniel Defoe's 1722 *Moll Flanders* (a female PICAROON), Mark Twain's 1884 *Huckleberry Finn*, to Aravind Adiga's 2008 *The White Tiger*. Cult film classics like *O Brother, Where Art Thou?* and *The Big Lebowski* brilliantly adapt the form. De-rascalising the picaro, as in *Forest Gump*, is one of many modern variants.

PICARESQUE TROPES include: MacGuffins Galore (to drive the action forward); Convenient Coincidences; The Narrow Escape Via Bedroom Window; The Elaborate Unnecessary Scheme; The Loyal Sidekick With a Questionable Benefits Package; The Fortune Immediately Squandered (Rich at Dawn, Broke by Dinner); The Moral Lesson Immediately Forgotten.

LOVE STORIES & ROMANCE
will they, won't they

LOVE STORIES explore romantic relationships alongside broader social and philosophical themes and issues of personal identity, emphasising psychological complexity and character development. Sadly, this often allows for ambiguous or unhappy endings. It is an ancient genre. *Adam and Eve* is one early love story that didn't go smoothly (traumatised offspring included). Here are some variants of the genre:

DOOMED LOVE portrays love as a transcendent force ultimately destroyed by external circumstances. The passionate connection between *Romeo and Juliet* is terminated by family feuds and fatal misunderstandings.

SENSUALECTUAL works posit physical passion as a pathway to deep psychological and philosophical awakening. Pioneered in the West through novels like D.H. Lawrence's 1928 *Lady Chatterley's Lover*.

CHICK LIT focuses on social pressures around relationships, careers, and female identity. Self-deprecating humour and misadventure drives the narrative. Named for Helen Fielding's 1996 *Bridget Jones's Diary*.

ROMANCE (or **GENRE ROMANCE**) is a trade category whose stories feature a central love story and an emotionally satisfying and optimistic ending. The romantic leads tend to meet early (the **MEET CUTE**), and experience sustained chemistry and attraction, overcoming obstacles to be together, 'happily ever after' (**HEA**) or 'happy for now' (**HFN**). Subgenres include:

HISTORICAL: Love stories set in past eras with period-accurate detail
PARANORMAL: Love stories with supernatural or magical elements.
SUSPENSE: Romance mixed with danger and thriller elements.

INSPIRATIONAL: Faith-based love stories emphasizing spiritual values.
EROTIC: Love stories with explicit sexual content.
BODICE RIPPER: Historical romances, popular in the 1970s and early 1980s. Named for images of torn bodices on the book covers, they are

… publishing's answer to the Big Mac: They are juicy, cheap, predictable, and devoured in stupefying quantities by legions of loyal fans. The Wall Street Journal, 1980.

In the US, romance accounts for around one quarter of all books sold. Love is serious business. Bollywood directors agree: *Masala* films (which blend multiple genres) almost always feature a central love story.

LOVE STORY TROPES include: *Class Divides; Lovers Separated by Historical Catastrophe; The Decades-Long Correspondence; A Fleeting Connection Never Forgotten; The Relationship Ruined by Success* (achievement as the antagonist of domestic happiness); *Intergenerational Echo* (kids must not repeat their parents' romantic mistakes); *Love Triangles with Ideological Corners* (choose between passion, stability, or doctoral thesis); *The Affair During Academic Sabbatical; Second Chance; Slow Burn.*

ROMANCE TROPES include: *The Meet Cute; Forbidden Love; Enemies to Lovers; Love at First Sight; The Makeover; The Love Triangle* (three people; two potential couples; one heartbreak); *Forced Proximity* (stranded, tied up etc); *Fake Relationship* (turns into love); *The Bodyguard; The Billionaire's Assistant; Grumpy vs. Sunshine* (annoyance deepens into attraction); *Secret Baby.*

The Thriller
action, tension, suspense

The **THRILLER** is a sprawling super-genre with a focus on action, tension, and suspense. Fast paced, with regular location changes, time crunches, moments of jeopardy, and cliffhangers, it has many variants:

CRIME OR MYSTERY THRILLERS: Solving a mystery or crime becomes a matter of life and death; e.g. Graham Greene's 1950 *The Third Man*.

POLITICAL THRILLERS unfold in worlds of conspiracies, power struggles, corruption, assassination, and scandal; e.g. *The Manchurian Candidate*.

SPY THRILLERS deal with the shadowy world of espionage, double agents, international intrigue, and webs of loyalty and betrayal. *The 39 Steps*.

PSYCHOLOGICAL THRILLERS focus on unstable mental states, psychological manipulation, gaslighting, etc.; e.g. Gillian Flynn's 2012 *Gone Girl*.

LEGAL THRILLERS see legal professionals fight to reveal the truth, facing dangerous adversaries in and out of the courtroom; e.g. *The Firm*.

DOMESTIC THRILLERS centre on threats within seemingly normal families or relationships; e.g. A.J. Finn's 2018 *The Woman in the Window*.

TECHNO THRILLERS involve technology (including biotechnology) as a significant plot element; e.g. Michael Crichton's 1990 *Jurassic Park*.

ACTION THRILLERS emphasise physical danger, chases, and confrontations, guns, explosions and all; e.g. R. Ludlum's 1980 *The Bourne Identity*.

The list of subgenres goes on. **SUPERNATURAL THRILLERS** have fantasy or horror elements. **ENVIRONMENTAL THRILLERS** focus on ecological threats. Then there are **CORPORATE THRILLERS**, high stakes **MILITARY THRILLERS**, exciting **MEDICAL THRILLERS**, and many more!

TYPICAL THRILLER PLOT BEATS: HERO *gets into trouble* → BIG TWIST *or double-cross* → BIG REVEAL *where we learn the bigger story behind it all* → BIG CHASE *or* FIGHT → JUSTICE *is finally delivered, at a price ...*

The tension in a thriller comes from escalating high stakes, uncertainty, threats, obstacles, time pressure, difficult choices, and disproportionate strength between the hero and the villain. Protagonists are typically:

> ... *an unwitting hero who is reluctantly drawn into the story and must do battle with an epic villain to save the lives of innocent victims. Our hero inevitably finds themself deeply involved with insane criminals— who will threaten, double-cross and kill anyone who stands in their way.* Eric R Williams, The Screenwriters Taxonomy.

Effective thriller writers manipulate tension through strategic timing— revealing enough to keep readers engaged, while delaying full disclosure (building suspense) until maximum emotional impact can be achieved.

THRILLER TROPES include: The Innocent Framed; The Expert Protagonist; Race Against Time; The Point of No Return (the protagonist is committed); The Shadow Organization (with unlimited reach); The Tainted Authority Figure (no more institutional support); The Conspiracy; The Secret Weapon; The McGuffin Exchange (a critical thing changes hands); The Cat and Mouse Game; The Unnecessarily Complex Death Trap; The Improbably Maintained Hairstyle (despite explosions and underwater escapes); The Ticking Bomb; The Villain Monologue (explains their entire plan); The Single-Use Disguise; The Final Twist.

CRIME FICTION
and true crime

Humans enjoy creating and breaking laws, and reading about criminal acts and their investigation. These stories invite us to root for law enforcers, or lawbreakers, or victims, while examining broader societal issues,

CRIME FICTION imagines a crime, the execution of that crime, its investigation, then concludes with revelations and resolution (justice and punishment). It is the most popular genre of fiction, accounting for 25–30% of sales (up to 45% in Scandinavia). Sub-genres include:

> **PRISON FICTION** is often set in prison, with themes of injustice and escape, e.g. Stephen King's 1982 *Rita Hayworth and Shawshank Redemption*.
>
> **ORGANIZED CRIME STORIES**: e.g. Mario Puzo's 1969 *The Godfather*.
>
> **HEIST/CAPER FICTION** revolves around elaborate criminal schemes and their execution, usually told from the criminals' viewpoint.
>
> **DETECTIVES AND MURDER MYSTERY** (*featured on page 44*).
>
> **PSYCHOLOGICAL CRIME FICTION** focuses on the mental states and internal landscapes of criminals, victims and investigators.
>
> **FIGHT FOR JUSTICE STORIES** examine systemic inequality and instances of legal injustice. They are often based on, or inspired by, true stories.

Henry Sutton, in *Crafting Crime Fiction*, lists four factors a crime writer should always consider: *Pace; Purpose; Menace; and Motivation*.

TRUE CRIME FICTION reimagines real crime through a fictional lens, blending factual events with creative writing. But turning a real tragedy into entertainment should be approached sensitively. Ask yourself:

> *... what story you are trying to tell and why, chase every avenue and speak to everyone willing to engage with you if you want to ensure that the work has integrity.* Prof. Whitney Phillips.

Blurring fact and fiction in real criminal cases was a mainstay of Victorian era 'Penny Dreadful' pamphlets. The investigation of the 1860 murder at Rode Hill House (depicted in Kate Summerscale's 2008 novel *The Suspicions of Mr Whicher*) was damaged irreparably by such coverage.

TRUE CRIME REPORTAGE presents factual accounts of criminal cases, examining motives, investigations, and societal impact. It has boomed in the 21st century, especially in TV and podcast. Whitney Phillips suggests people are drawn to feel invested in the outcome of something *real*, or to process anxieties around their own vulnerability to violent crime. Truman Capote's 1965 true crime non-fiction novel *In Cold Blood* sits somewhere between reportage and fiction.

CRIME FICTION TROPES: 19TH CENTURY: The Criminogenic Environment; The Criminal Confession Letter; The Fallen Woman's Redemption; The Class-Crossing Disguise; The Prison Reform Crusader; The Corrupted Inheritance; The Tainted Legacy. 20TH CENTURY: Urban Decay as Character; Heist Gone Wrong; Prison Break; The Criminal Code of Honour; The Reluctant Accomplice; The Criminal Family Dynasty; The New Identity. 21ST CENTURY: The Digital Evidence Trail; The Traumatized Investigator; The True Crime Podcast Tie-In; The Unreliable Surveillance Footage; The Cold Case DNA Resolution; The Corruption Goes Deeper.

Detectives & Whodunnits
all will be revealed

DETECTIVE FICTION drills deep into the unique methods, character, and personal lives of crime solvers. Often titular members of the police force, 'detectives' come in all shapes and sizes, with many shades in between:

THOUGHTFUL PROS or **AMATEUR** investigators, (journalists, academics, or everyday citizens), who rely on intelligence and experience.
NOIR FIGURES, whose psychological complexity stems from past traumas that haunt investigations, often leading to ambiguous resolutions.
HARD-BOILED violence-hardened detectives, who navigate corrupt urban landscapes with terse dialogue and personal moral codes.
HISTORICAL crime solvers, operating within specific historical periods.
SCIENTIFIC types, like forensic experts or medical examiners.

The analytical detective, using scientific methods and deductive reasoning emerges with Edgar Allen Poe's 1841 *The Murders in the Rue Morgue*. The *Sherlock Holmes* stories by Conan Doyle [1887–1927] then established the Eccentric Genius Detective archetype that influenced all subsequent sleuthing.

MURDER MYSTERIES involve reader/viewer participation. As the mystery progresses towards a Climactic Revelation, we must deduce the killer's identity (**WHODUNIT**), the method (**HOWDUNIT**), and even why the crime occurred (**WHYDUNIT**)? The format dominated the Golden Age of detective fiction (c.1920–1939), when writers like Agatha Christie and Dorothy L. Sayers established conventions around clues, red herrings, and dramatic reveals:

1. The **CRIMINAL** *is mentioned in the early part of the story.*
2. *All supernatural or* **PRETERNATURAL AGENCIES** *are ruled out.*

3. Not more than one SECRET ROOM or *passage is allowable.*
4. No hitherto undiscovered POISONS *may be used.*
5. Accident or unaccountable INTUITION *must not help the detective.*
6. The DETECTIVE *must not themself commit the crime.*
7. All CLUES *are produced for the inspection of the reader* (FAIR-PLAY).
8. TWINS *must not appear unless we have been duly prepared for them.*
9. The detective's 'WATSON' *figure must not conceal any thoughts; and their intelligence must be very slightly below that of the average reader.*

The moral outrage at murder, the intrigue of the puzzle, and the catharsis of revelation and resolution all contribute to the success of this genre.

DETECTIVE FICTION TROPES include: 19TH CENTURY: *The Criminal Mastermind; The Loyal Chronicler or Side-kick; Opium Den Research Trip.* MODERN: *The Client Never Tells The Whole Truth; Functional Alcoholism Superpower* (investigative abilities improve with each drink); *Cold Opening; Everyone Has A Motive; Case-Solving Concussion* (head wound leads to breakthrough); *The Dramatically Lit Office* (Venetian blinds aid progress). MURDER MYSTERY: *The Butler; The Victim Nobody Mourns; The Red Herring Factory* (everyone lurking/muttering/handling daggers); *The Isolated Country Mansion; More Secret Passages Than Walls; The Hobby That Solves Everything* (e.g. detective's obscure interest in 17th-century Romanian shoelaces); *Elaborate Murder Method; Implausible Murder Rate* (in small village); *The Dying Message; The Gathering.*

Young Adult
teenage kicks

Young Adult Fiction, **YA** for short, has protagonists similar in age to its teenage readership, and their actions and decisions take centre stage in the narrative. Plot lines are relatively uncomplicated and narrative voice tends towards an adolescent's world view, immersed in contemporary youth culture and technology. Stories are usually only 200–300 pages and overlap significantly with **Coming of Age** (*see page 15*). The subgenres are legion—almost every literary genre has a young adult version.

Whereas children's literature tends to present readers with a closed moral universe, in which the bad are punished and the good rewarded, YA fiction calls such assumptions into question. *The Young Adult Canon* describes how these stories:

> *… interrogate social constructions, foregrounding the relationship between the society and the individual, and tackle difficult, oftentimes adult, issues that arise during an adolescent's journey toward identity.* Victor Malo-Juvera & Crag Hill

The central YA character is usually a teenager, exceptional in some way, be it their ability to exercise empathy, read social situations, or because they are an 'outsider'. Their intense emotionality, first time experiences, and increasing independence all contribute to their character development, as fundamental questions are posed, explicitly or thematically.

Skaz, a literary technique characterized by a first-person narration that mimics spontaneous speech, is a strong feature in YA. It incorporates *age-specific slang* and *neologisms*, as well as *fragmented syntax* and *run-on sentences*, not to mention *upspeak* and *vocal fry*, with *discourse markers* ("like," "literally," "I mean"), lashed with *emotional intensity* and *hyperbole*, and even *code-switching* (language changes with the audience, peers vs. adults).

Distinctive teen voices, like Holden Caulfield in J.D. Salinger's *The Catcher in the Rye*, Christopher Boone in Mark Haddon's *The Curious Incident of the Dog in the Night-Time*, and Starr Carter in *The Hate U Give* by Angie Thomas, create immediacy and authenticity, allowing readers to experience the unfiltered perspective of a teenage narrator.

In recent years the genre has garnered increasing interest and respect in the literary and cinematic worlds. Digital platforms have been accelerants to this fire. Screen adaptations of works such as *The Fault in Our Stars* and *13 Reasons Why* have been hugely successful. The genre is also undergoing 'adultification'—in 2024 Harper Collins found that more than a quarter of YA readers were over the age of 28. The boundaries have perhaps always been blurry (e.g. Harper Lee's *To Kill a Mockingbird*).

YOUNG ADULT TROPES include: **Good vs. Evil** and **Right vs. Wrong** (and the grey area in between). **Adults as Adversaries** (repressive old guards). **First love** (Bittersweet); **Paranormal Romance** (with elves or vampires); **Emotional Rollercoasters**; **Talismanic Objects** (good luck charms/love tokens/journals/mementos); **Absent Parents**; **The Outsider** (the protagonist does not 'fit in' to some aspect of the world around them); **Found Family**; **Chosen One** (ordinary teen with extraordinary destiny); **Love Triangles**; **Instant Maturity** (teens take on adult responsibilities); **Hidden Powers**; **Secret Identity**; **Mysterious Past**; **Boarding School** (and other closed environments); **Tournaments** (with real peril); **Resistance**.

Children's Fiction
once upon a time

What were your favourite stories growing up? Ask that question to someone and watch their face light up as they think back to those magical works, like recalling old friends. As adults, **CHILDREN'S FICTION** can seem too simple—in vocabulary, story and allegory—but the best ones always transcend the genre, as C.S. Lewis notes:

> I am almost inclined to set it up as a canon that a children's story which is enjoyed only by children is a bad children's story. On Three Ways of Writing for Children, 1952.

Since the era of mass book printing began, notions of childhood have evolved (and continue to do so). Early works, aimed at children in the Christianised world, such as the 1845 German collection *Struwwelpeter* by Heinrich Hoffman, tended towards **MORAL INSTRUCTION**. Enid Blyton professed a similar (less violently executed) aim to:

> …give children a feeling of security as well as pleasure – they know that they will never find anything wrong, hideous, horrible, murderous or vulgar in my books, although there is always plenty of excitement, mystery and fun… I am not out only to tell stories… I am out to inculcate decent thinking, loyalty, honesty, kindliness, and all the things that children should be taught. Enid Blyton

Roald Dahl is the master of the more modern approach, rooted in empathy and aiming to delight rather than obviously instruct:

> If you want to remember what it's like to live in a child's world, you've got to get down on your hands and knees and live like that for a week. You find you have to look up at all these bloody giants around you who are always telling you what to do and what not to do … children absolutely warm to this. Roald Dahl

Perry Nodelman argues that children's literature:

> ... is written in a SIMPLE STYLE, with a focus on ACTION rather than description, and a MATTER-OF-FACT TONE despite the strangeness of the events. CHILD PROTAGONISTS focalise through a CHILD'S PERSPECTIVE to create a DUAL PERSPECTIVE (child viewpoint and adult narrator). The simplicity often masks HIDDEN COMPLEXITIES. For example, INNOCENCE and the acquisition OF KNOWLEDGE are central themes, as is a pervasive sense of NOSTALGIA, often centralised around ideas of HOME and LEAVING HOME.

Writers of children's literature need to get the vocabulary right: too easy and it will feel patronising, too hard and it might alienate. For very young readers, RHYME, REPETITION, and CALL AND RESPONSE are important ingredients in the mix.

KID'S LIT TROPES include: Child Hero; Anthropomorphism, especially Talking Animals (Beatrix Potter, The Wind in the Willows, The Wizard of Oz), but also Trains and Cars; Goodies and Baddies (clear moral distinctions); Pourquoi? (kids ask big questions, and answers can be mythical, e.g. Kipling's Just So Stories); Magical Objects; Magical Helpers; Magic Doorways; The Quest or Journey; Hidden Worlds; Home Sweet Home (often after a really big Adventure); Absent parents; Change and transition (coping with, embracing, and processing change as part of Growing Up, e.g. J.M. Barrie's Peter and Wendy); Smarter Than The Adults; Triumph of the Smallest; Repetition, Repetition, Repetition (repeated phrases, rhyming poetry); Transformation (frogs to princes); Overcoming Fears; The Power of Friendship.

Biography & Memoir
all about a person

A **biography** is a detailed overview of a person's life. A huge genre in non-fiction, it may be chronological or thematic in the way it is organised, and focus on the subject's outer life, inner life or both. Biographers use literary techniques to create a gripping narrative, and go to great lengths to understand their principal. In his 2012 study of the biographical art, *Footsteps*, Richard Holmes literally follows in his subjects' footsteps.

There are two main approaches: **Autopsy** dissects and analyses a life, to reveal the 'real person' beneath the public image, often focusing on tragic individuals (Kurt Cobain, Sylvia Plath), while **Portraiture** presents a more cohesive and recognisable image of a person, including:

> *... how they affected and influenced people, what their friendships were like, how they were one thing to one person and another thing to another person* Hermione Lee.

Biopics like *The Imitation Game* and *Oppenheimer* are portraiture adaptations which at times move away from fact in the service of a gripping movie.

Autobiography is a self-penned account of the author's own life. Agatha Christie's posthumously published autobiography is a fine example:

> *Difficult to know what one's first memory is. I remember distinctly my third birthday. The sense of my own importance surges up in me ... Three candles.*

Memoir is a form of autobiographical writing which focuses on a particular period in the author's life. Roald Dahl's *Boy* describes childhood; Will Carruthers' 2016 *Playing the Bass with Three Left Hands* is a **Music Memoir** set in the 1980s and early 1990s. Memoir can be more visceral than any novel; e.g. Jeanette Winterson's *Why be Happy When You Can be Normal?*

Travel & Nature
moving through space and time

Travel writing describes an author's experience of places and cultures beyond their usual environment. **Literary travelogues** like Bruce Chatwin's 1987 *The Songlines* blend research with personal journey. **Immersive Travel Journalism**, such as Katherine Boo's 2012 *Behind the Beautiful Forevers*, fuses extended stays with factual reporting. **Adventure narratives** recount expeditions or misadventures with suspenseful pacing. Jon Krakauer's 1997 *Into Thin Air*, based on a tragic ascent of Mount Everest, is both compelling and heartbreaking.

History, architecture, crafts, food, decor, fashion, culture, medicine, geology, botany, and zoology all have a role in good travel writing, and sometimes one of these will dominate, as in **Historical travelogues**. William Dalrymple's 1993 *City of Djinns* combines historical research and contemporary observation with metaphor, imagery, pacing, and voice.

Nature writing elevates observation of the natural world to a literary art, combining descriptions of plants, animals, and environments with observations about humanity's place within ecosystems. Early examples of the genre include Henry David Thoreau's 1854 *Walden*, and Hermann Hesse's 1920 *Wandering*.

> Visual affinities of colour, relief and texture abound. A fallen branch echoes the deltoid form of a streambed into which it has come to rest. Chrome yellow autumn elm leaves find their colour rhyme in the eye-ring of the blackbird.
>
> Robert Macfarlane, The Wild Places, 2007.

HISTORY
everything has one

HISTORY WRITING has been around a long time, from Herodotus [c. 484–425 BC] to Sima Qian [c. 145–86 BC] and Josephus [37–100 CE]. But while early historians recorded the deeds of kings and the outcomes of battles, modern ones delve into the histories of, well, almost everything:

MILITARY HISTORY: Wars, battles, weapons, military institutions.
POLITICAL HISTORY: Governments, policy, and power struggles.
ECONOMIC HISTORY: Economic systems, trade and institutions.
SOCIAL HISTORY: Everyday lives, social structures, and movements.
CULTURAL HISTORY: Beliefs, customs, and cultural expressions.
INTELLECTUAL HISTORY: Ideas, philosophies, and scientific thought.
NATURAL HISTORY: Evolution of the universe, geology, environment.
GENDER HISTORY: Gender in society and institutions over time.
MICROHISTORY: Narrow focus, on an event, community or profession.
COMMODITY HISTORY: One item, e.g. salt, silk, chickens, ink, peanuts.
TECH HISTORY: Science, technology, and manufacturing.

Works of non-fiction can be literary masterpieces in their own right, e.g. Orlando Figes' 2002 *Natasha's Dance, a cultural history of Russia* hones in on art, literature, and collective identity. Their sweep can also be epic, as in **GRAND NARRATIVES**; e.g. David Graeber's 2011 *Debt: The First 5,000 Years* or Jared Diamond's 1997 *Guns, Germs, and Steel* which explores 13,000 years of history, posing big questions in a matter-of-fact style:

> ...why were Europeans, rather than Africans or Native Americans, the ones to end up with guns, the nastiest germs, and steel? Guns, Germs, and Steel, 1997

CURRENT AFFAIRS
what's happening

We all enjoy discussing the present—who is up, who is down, the issues of the day. Literary non-fiction works covering current affairs fall into various categories, mirroring the histories opposite. From sport to bitcoin, the state of schools to plastic pollution, there is a book on it.

POLITICS: Personal and investigative; e.g. Anne Applebaum's 2020 *Twilight of Democracy*, which explores the rise of authoritarianism in the West.
POLICY ANALYSIS explores current laws, policies and their impacts.

GEOPOLITICS: Samuel Huntington's 1996 *The Clash of Civilisations* and Chimamanda Ngozi Adichie's 2014 *We Should All Be Feminists* drill into global power structures and contrasting value systems.

THE ECONOMY: Creative works like Mark Fisher's 2009 *Capitalist Realism* look at how economic systems infiltrate cultural consciousness, limiting our ability to envision alternatives to the dominant order.

SOCIOCULTURAL: E.g. Ta-Nehisi Coates' 2015 *Between the World and Me* and John Berger's 1972 *Ways of Seeing*, exploring how aesthetics interacts with political consciousness. Also music, art.

ISSUE BASED: Works centred on present issues like climate change, inequality, technology, policing; e.g. Naomi Klein's 2014 *This Changes Everything: Capitalism vs. the Climate*.

CRISIS CHRONICLE: Detailed accounts of crises (environmental, medical, educational, sport).

Popular Science
intellectual growth

Popular Science translates scientific ideas into accessible narratives for a general readership. From mathematics (James Gleick's 1987 *Chaos*), to cosmology (Brian Greene's 1999 *The Elegant Universe*), to biology (Mary Roach's 2013 *Gulp: Adventures on the Alimentary Canal*) to geology (Robert Hazen's 2012 *The Story of Earth*), to linguistics (Susie Dent' 2016 *Modern Tribes*), and materials science (Ed Conway's 2023 *Material World*), the genre offers an engaging way to catch up on human knowledge.

> *In six thousand years, you could never grow wings on a reptile. With sixty million, however, you could have feathers, too.* John McPhee, Annals of the Former World, 1998.

Science writers use many literary devices to deliver their goods, blending biography, history, intrigue, suspense, descriptive prose, and visits to rare places and boffins. Sometimes the science can play second fiddle to poetic historical narrative. Dava Sobel's 1993 global bestseller *Longitude* tells the story of marine clock inventor John Harrison, a man who

> *tested the waters of space-time. [...] He wrested the world's whereabouts from the stars, and locked the secret in a pocket watch.* Dava Sobel, Longitude, 1993

Major developments in science, like the AI revolution, tend to generate swathes of books warning against or championing them. Indeed ideas presented in popular science sometimes gain more traction with the public than with scientists; e.g. Elaine Morgan's *Aquatic Ape*.

Mind, Body, Spirit
spiritual growth

Over a third of the non-fiction book market deals with self-development, physical and mental health, spirituality, and religion.

Religious and Spiritual texts, like the Bible, Quran, Bhagavad Gita, Dhammapada, Tao Te Ching, and Yi Ching, are the bestselling books of all time, even today. More recent works translate ancient spiritual practices via metaphors and anecdote for the modern reader, e.g. Thich Nhat Hanh's 1975 *The Miracle Of Mindfulness*.

Mind Body Spirit texts present ancient ideas in a more personal and modern manner, whether it is breath, yoga, mindfulness, healing, channelling, psychic skills, death, spirits, past lives, psychedelics, dreams, or divination. Eckhart Tolle's 1997 *The Power of Now* is a good example of timeless concepts reimagined in accessible non-religious language.

The **Self Help** genre presents practical tools to help improve your motivation, confidence, productivity, finances, career success, work-life balance, relationships, sport performance, sex life, energy levels, mood, or waistline. Books like Susan Jeffers' 1987 *Feel the Fear and Do It Anyway* or James Clear's 2018 *Atomic Habits* use personal anecdotes and clear steps to help readers overcome their limitations. Personal **Auto Self Help** narratives explain how a solution helped the author overcome a problem.

Popular Psychology evolved from works like Viktor Frankl's 1946 *Man's Search for Meaning*, and Carl Jung's 1964 *Man and His Symbols*, which emphasised integration and connection. More modern examples include Daniel Kahneman's 2011 *Thinking, Fast and Slow*, Chris Voss's 2016 *Never Split the Difference,* and Mihaly Csikszentmihalyi's 1990 *Flow*.

LITERARY FORMS
the long and short of it

THE PLAY as a literary form dates back over 2500 years to Ancient Greece, India and China. Most ancient plays were written in **METRE**, and 2,000 years later Shakespeare was still writing drama in **VERSE** (rhyming iambic pentameter) or **BLANK VERSE** (unrhymed iambic pentameter). Sometimes a character speaks in **PROSE** (no meter) to signal lower social class, distress, or lack of pretension (Hamlet speaks prose to the gravediggers). Plays are often divided into **ACTS** to allow scene changes. There were five acts from Roman times to Shakespeare's day, three by the 19th century, and mostly two today. Very few modern plays employ verse, **OPERA** and **MUSICAL** being the exception. [typically 5,000-10,000 words, 60-120 pages]

THE NOVEL form appears in the 1st and 2nd centuries CE, with Greek and Latin prose works such as *Daphnis and Chloe* by Longus, and *The Golden Ass* by Apuleius. The first modern novel is considered to be *The Tale of the Genji* by Murasaki Shikibu (Japan, c.1010). It returns to Europe with Miguel de Cervantes' 1605 *Don Quixote*, followed by Aphra Behn's 1688 *Oroonoko*, Daniel Defoe's 1719 *Robinson Crusoe*, Samuel Richardson's 1740 *Pamela*, and others. [typically 50,000-110,000 words, 180-400 pages]

THE NOVELLA is a baby novel, but not necessarily easier to write. Saying a lot in few words takes skill; some writers consider it the perfect form:

> *... the beautiful daughter of a rambling, bloated, ill-shaven giant (but a giant who's a genius on his best days).* Ian McEwan, New Yorker 2012

John Steinbeck's 1937 *Of Mice and Men* is an excellent example. It tells a complete narrative within a tight frame with fully fledged characters and